DAMON DU BRUYN

# Beyond Revenue

*How Smart Businesses Unlock Profit Others Miss*

*First edition*

*This book was professionally typeset on Reedsy.*
*Find out more at reedsy.com*

*For the entrepreneurs who grind every day.*
*For the ones who know the system is rigged against them — but choose to win anyway.*
*For those who understand that growth without profit is a mirage.*
*This book is for you — the operators, the wolves, the ones who protect what's theirs.*

"Revenue is vanity. Profit is sanity.
Cash is reality."

Authors,
Damon Du Bruyn & Jordan Anderson

# Contents

# Foreword

Most entrepreneurs chase revenue. They brag about sales, headcount, and "growth," but behind the curtain, their businesses are bleeding margin. They don't see the leaks, the inefficiencies, the waste — until it's too late.

That's why this book matters. *The Invisible Margin* isn't another theory-filled business book. It's a tool. It reveals the traps, the leaks, and the habits that silently destroy profit. More importantly, it gives you the systems, tools, and mindset to patch those leaks and unlock the margin already hiding in your business.

What separates businesses that survive from those that collapse isn't size or even innovation. It's discipline. It's the relentless focus on profit. That's the message of this book — and if you read with focus, it will change not just your numbers, but the way you operate.

# Preface

We wrote this book because too many entrepreneurs are chasing the wrong goal. They chase revenue. They chase attention. They chase scale. But none of that matters if there's no profit margin.

Profit is survival. Profit is freedom. Profit is what lets you build, scale, and seize opportunities when others are collapsing. Yet most businesses leave profit on the table every day. They bleed through leaks, inefficiencies, poor pricing, and weak discipline.

*The Invisible Margin* is here to change that. It's not fluff. It's not motivational hype. It's a playbook — tested strategies, systems, and audits you can implement immediately to capture hidden profit. I've seen companies double their margins not by selling more, but by simply tightening the leaks they never noticed.

This book is my attempt to hand you those tools — so you can stop bleeding, start capturing, and build a business that thrives in any environment.

# Acknowledgments

No one builds alone.

To the entrepreneurs who shared their numbers and their struggles — thank you for exposing the reality most books ignore. Your stories shaped the lessons in these pages.

To our mentors and peers who taught us the ruthless discipline of protecting margin — your insights sharpened this playbook.

And to the reader: thank you for betting on yourself. Most will keep chasing vanity. You chose to chase sanity. That choice is why you'll win.

# 1

# The Profit Mirage

Most business owners brag about revenue. They love to say, *"We did seven figures this year"* or *"We hit $500k last quarter."* Revenue is sexy. It looks good on paper, impresses investors, and feeds the ego.

But here's the hard truth: **revenue is a vanity metric. Profit is the only metric that matters.**

## 1. Why Revenue Lies

Revenue tells you how much money came in. It doesn't tell you how much stayed. A business can do $1 million in revenue and still be losing money. In fact, according to a CB Insights study, **38% of businesses fail because they run out of cash — not because they lack revenue.**

A "successful" top-line often hides a collapsing bottom-line. Growth without margin is a treadmill — faster and faster but never getting ahead.

☞ **Operator's move: Stop asking, *"What's our revenue?"* Start asking, *"What's our operating profit margin?"***

## 2. The Illusion of Scale

Many entrepreneurs think scaling solves everything. "If I just get more customers, profit will come." Wrong.

If your unit economics are broken — if each customer costs $120 to acquire and only brings $100 in profit — scaling actually **multiplies your losses.** That's why so many startups implode after raising millions. They scaled the problem.

Harvard Business Review found that **companies with healthy margins survive downturns 3x more often** than high-revenue, low-margin peers. Margin is resilience.

☞ **Operator's move: Before chasing growth, audit your unit economics. Are you making or losing money per customer? Fix the leaks first.**

## 3. The Margin Lens

The elite don't measure success in revenue. They measure in **margins per unit of effort.**

- **Gross margin:** Profit after cost of goods sold (COGS).
- **Operating margin:** Profit after operating expenses.
- **Net margin:** The bottom line after everything.

Amazon is famous for razor-thin net margins — yet Bezos focused relentlessly on **cash flow per share**, not vanity metrics. That lens kept Amazon alive while competitors bled out.

☞ **Operator's move: Pick one key margin metric and track it weekly. Treat it like your heartbeat.**

## 4. Common Profit Mirages

1. **Discounting to drive sales** – Looks like growth, destroys margin.
2. **Bloated product lines** – More SKUs = more complexity = hidden costs.
3. **High churn masked by new sales** – Top-line looks flat, profit evaporates.
4. **Overstaffing too early** – Adds fixed cost before profit justifies it.
5. **Tool creep** – $29/month tools stack into thousands with no ROI.

☞ **Operator's move: Every "growth hack" you chase must be run through the margin filter. If it doesn't protect or increase profit, kill it.**

## 5. The Reality of Cash vs Profit

Here's the kicker: even profit doesn't always mean survival. Cash does. You can be profitable on paper but die from cash timing issues (slow receivables, fast payables).

That's why **cash flow statements matter more than income statements.** As the saying goes: "Revenue is vanity, profit is sanity, cash is reality."

☞ **Operator's move: Build a cash flow dashboard. Track inflows, outflows, and timing. A profitable but cash-starved business is still fragile.**

## 6. Quick Profit Reset (Do This in 7 Days)

1. Calculate your **gross, operating, and net margins.**
2. Rank your products/services by margin, not revenue.
3. Identify your bottom 20% of customers (low spend, high support). Decide if you cut, increase pricing, or redesign terms.
4. Audit your last 90 days of expenses — cut tools or subscriptions with no ROI.
5. Review receivables: how many days are you waiting for cash?

These moves alone can add 5–10% to your bottom line without a single new customer.

*Final words:*

The herd chases revenue because it looks impressive. Wolves chase profit because it buys freedom.

Revenue without margin is a mirage — it looks like water, but it leaves you thirsty. Profit is the real oasis. Build your business to protect it, grow it, and multiply it.

The hunt doesn't start with "more." It starts with **keeping what's already yours.**

# 2

# The Hidden Leaks

A business doesn't usually collapse from one big mistake. It dies from a thousand small leaks. Tiny inefficiencies, overlooked fees, and creeping expenses quietly bleed away margin until the bottom line disappears.

Most entrepreneurs never see these leaks because they're focused on growth. But growth without control is gasoline on a fire. If you don't find and patch the leaks, every new customer just makes the problem worse.

## 1. Subscription Creep

One of the biggest modern killers of margin is **tool sprawl.** Every SaaS looks cheap — $29 here, $49 there — but over a year, even 10 unused tools can cost thousands. Multiply that across a team, and suddenly you're leaking 3–5% of revenue into software no one uses.

☞ **Operator's Move: Run a tool audit every 90 days. Kill or consolidate anything that isn't used weekly or generating measurable ROI.**

## 2. Payment Processing Fees

Most businesses treat payment processing fees as "the cost of doing business." Wrong. A 2.9% card fee on $1M revenue = **$29,000 gone**. For low-margin businesses, that's life or death.

There are alternatives: ACH, RTP, or even negotiating blended rates with processors like Stripe, PayPal, or Square once volume passes certain thresholds.

☞ **Operator's Move: Shift 20–30% of transactions off cards to cheaper rails. Savings drop straight to the bottom line.**

## 3. Inventory & Waste

Retail and e-commerce businesses bleed margin on overstocking, spoilage, or holding costs. Even service businesses suffer from "inventory" in the form of unused labor hours.

Walmart runs inventory with near-military precision. They know exactly how long cash is tied up in product. That's why they crush competitors on margin.

☞ **Operator's Move: Track inventory turnover ratio. Dead stock = dead profit. Free cash trapped in shelves.**

## 4. Labor Inefficiency

Payroll is usually the largest expense. But many businesses carry "phantom staff" — roles that don't directly create or protect profit. Add meetings, misalignment, or weak accountability, and labor costs balloon while output stagnates.

According to McKinsey, companies lose **20–30% of revenue annually to inefficiency.** That's not revenue lost to competitors — it's wasted internally.

☞ **Operator's Move: Apply the 80/20 test to labor. Which roles and activities produce 80% of the profit impact? Everything else must be automated, outsourced, or eliminated.**

## 5. Energy & Utility Costs

Hidden leaks aren't always digital. Restaurants, warehouses, and offices quietly bleed through inefficient energy use, unmonitored utility bills, or poor maintenance. One chain of grocery stores saved $2M annually simply by switching to LED lighting and negotiating bulk energy contracts.

☞ **Operator's Move: Run a utility audit annually. Negotiate rates, upgrade systems, and eliminate waste.**

## 6. Marketing Waste

Marketing is vital, but poorly tracked campaigns are a profit black hole. Google and Meta ads eat billions in wasted spend because businesses chase impressions, not ROI.

**☞ Operator's Move: Audit Customer Acquisition Cost (CAC) vs Lifetime Value (LTV). If CAC > 20–30% of LTV, you're leaking. Kill campaigns that don't pay.**

## 7. The Leverage Blind Spot

Many entrepreneurs overpay for capital — expensive loans, high-interest credit, or equity dilution. They see money coming in, but miss how much is leaking out through financing costs.

**☞ Operator's Move: Always compare capital costs. Refinancing or restructuring can save thousands annually.**

## 8. The Silent Leak: Time

The most invisible leak of all: wasted time. Every unproductive meeting, every hour spent on non-critical tasks is a hidden cost. Time is the only expense you can't recover.

Elon Musk once said, *"Meetings are a trap unless they are short, focused, and necessary.*" Time discipline is profit discipline.

☞ **Operator's Move: Audit your calendar. If it doesn't drive revenue, protect margin, or build strategy, delete it.**

## 9. How to Hunt Leaks

Run a **Leak Audit** once per quarter:

1. List your top 10 expenses.
2. For each, ask: *Is this generating measurable ROI?*
3. Cut, consolidate, or renegotiate anything that fails.
4. Track savings — roll them directly into profit or reinvest into high-margin growth.

*Final words:*

The herd bleeds from leaks they never see. They shrug at fees, ignore waste, and treat inefficiency as normal. Wolves don't. Wolves hunt leaks with precision and patch them ruthlessly.

Because margin is life. And in the hunt for profit, every drop counts.

# 3

# Operational Hygiene

A business doesn't fall apart overnight. It rots slowly from neglect. Just like personal health, your company needs hygiene — small, repeatable practices that keep it lean, disciplined, and sharp.

The herd ignores hygiene. They chase the next sale, the next marketing tactic, the next "big move," while inefficiencies and waste quietly grow. By the time they notice, their margins are already gone.

Operators know better. They install hygiene systems early. They create processes that protect profit without needing constant attention. Hygiene isn't glamorous, but it's the difference between a fragile hustle and a resilient machine.

## 1. Standard Operating Procedures (SOPs)

Chaos kills margin. Every time a task is done differently, mistakes multiply, time drags, and quality drops. SOPs create consistency, and consistency creates efficiency.

McDonald's didn't scale because of great hamburgers. They scaled because every process — from flipping patties to cleaning floors — was standardized. That operational hygiene made them unstoppable.

☞ **Operator's Move: Document your top 10 recurring tasks (sales calls, onboarding, payroll, reporting). Make each repeatable. SOPs are your silent margin protectors.**

## 2. The 80/20 Rule in Processes

Not every process deserves equal attention. The **Pareto Principle (80/20)** shows that 20% of processes drive 80% of results.

Example: In a SaaS business, customer onboarding may be only 10% of time spent but 70% of churn risk. Tightening that process adds more margin than tinkering with less critical workflows.

☞ **Operator's Move: Identify the "critical 20%" of processes. Streamline, automate, and perfect those first.**

## 3. Communication Hygiene

Slack, email, and meetings bleed time — the most expensive resource. Without hygiene, communication becomes noise.

A Harvard Business Review study found employees lose **23 hours per week in unnecessary meetings.** That's more than half a workweek wasted.

☞ **Operator's Move:**

- **Set meeting rules: agenda first, timer running, outcome required.**
- **Move updates to dashboards instead of calls.**
- **Default to async unless live discussion is critical.**

**Clean communication = clean margin.**

## 4. Financial Hygiene

Financial sloppiness kills businesses silently. Late invoicing, poor collections, and unclear expense tracking — all eat into margin.

A U.S. Bank study found **82% of small business failures stem from poor cash flow management.** That's not a marketing issue. It's hygiene.

☞ **Operator's Move:**

- **Send invoices same-day, not "later."**

- **Enforce payment terms with automation.**
- **Run monthly expense reviews — every dollar must have a reason.**

## 5. Tech Hygiene

Tools multiply like weeds. One employee adds a new app, another signs up for a trial, and suddenly your tech stack is bloated, fragmented, and costly.

☞ **Operator's Move:**

- **Consolidate tools where possible (e.g., one CRM instead of three).**
- **Run quarterly tech audits — cut what doesn't deliver ROI.**
- **Enforce approval for all new software spend.**

Tech should sharpen margins, not strangle them.

## 6. Talent Hygiene

A-players drive margin. C-players drain it. Without hygiene, teams get bloated with mediocrity.

Netflix operates with a **"keeper test"**: if a manager wouldn't fight to keep someone, they let them go. Ruthless? Yes.

Effective? Absolutely.

☞ **Operator's Move:**

- **Regularly review team contribution vs cost.**
- **Cut slow performers quickly.**
- **Invest in A-players who multiply efficiency.**

## 7. Audit Hygiene

Operators don't trust assumptions. They audit. Not once a year. Continuously.

Toyota's legendary lean system thrives on **Kaizen** — constant improvement. Every process is tested, refined, improved. That hygiene is why Toyota cars last decades.

☞ **Operator's Move:**

- **Run a quarterly margin audit (revenues, expenses, leaks).**
- **Track KPIs weekly (gross margin %, customer churn, CAC).**
- **Build a dashboard so hygiene is visible, not theoretical.**

## 8. Daily Operator Hygiene

Three daily habits protect operational margin:

1. **Morning check:** Review one key metric daily (cash, margin, or sales).
2. **End-of-day review:** Write tomorrow's #1 priority before shutting down.
3. **Calendar hygiene:** Cut one useless meeting every week.

These micro-moves compound into serious profit protection.

*Final words:*

Hygiene isn't glamorous. The herd ignores it because they'd rather chase hype. That's why the herd fails.

Wolves respect hygiene. They know systems don't erode overnight — they erode daily if left unchecked. Hygiene isn't about being perfect. It's about being disciplined enough to protect profit every single day.

Your business is either compounding efficiency or compounding waste. Hygiene decides which.

# 4

# Pricing Power

Revenue grows slowly. Costs are hard to cut. But a single change in pricing can transform your bottom line overnight. A **1% increase in price** can boost profits by **8–12%** depending on the business model (McKinsey study). That's leverage no other move comes close to.

Yet most entrepreneurs under price. They chase customers by being "affordable," afraid of scaring people away. But in reality, weak pricing signals weak value — and kills your margin.

## 1. The Myth of Competing on Price

If your only advantage is being cheaper, you're already dead. Amazon doesn't just compete on price — they compete on speed, convenience, and trust. Apple doesn't compete on price at all — they sell identity and experience.

Low prices attract low-value customers. They churn faster, complain louder, and drain resources. High-value customers care about outcomes, not discounts.

☞ **Operator's Move: Stop being the cheapest option. Be the most valuable.**

## 2. The Psychology of Pricing

Pricing isn't math. It's psychology. Customers rarely know the "fair" price — they judge based on anchors, comparisons, and perceived value.

- **Anchoring:** Show a higher "premium" option to make your main product look affordable.
- **Charm pricing:** $97 feels psychologically smaller than $100.
- **Decoy effect:** Add a mid-tier option to drive customers to the higher margin plan.

☞ **Operator's Move: Reframe your offers. Don't just change numbers — change perception.**

## 3. Premium vs. Commodity

There are only two profitable positions in any market: **the cheapest** or **the premium.** Everyone stuck in the middle gets squeezed.

- Walmart thrives by owning "cheapest."

- Rolex thrives by owning "premium."
- Mid-tier watch brands? Forgotten.

☞ **Operator's Move: Decide your lane. If you're not the absolute cheapest, raise your positioning and own premium.**

## 4. Value-Based Pricing

Cost-plus pricing ("I'll charge 20% over my costs") is lazy. Billionaires use **value-based pricing** — charging based on the outcome delivered.

Example: A consultant who helps a company earn $1M in new revenue shouldn't charge $100.

# 5

# The Cost of Complexity

Most entrepreneurs believe more is better. More products, more services, more offers. But complexity is the silent killer of profit. Every extra SKU, feature, or service line adds hidden costs — storage, training, support, management — that erode margin.

The world's strongest businesses win by **simplifying**, not multiplying. They strip down to what works and run it with precision. The herd spreads themselves thin. The wolves sharpen their edge.

## 1. Why Complexity Destroys Margin

- **Inventory Bloat:** More products = more stock, more cash trapped, higher holding costs.
- **Training Costs:** Each new service requires more employee training.
- **Customer Confusion:** Too many options reduce conversion. A Harvard study showed that **choice overload drops sales**

by 30%.
- **Operational Drag:** Complexity slows decision-making and execution.

☞ **Operator's Move: Every new offer must earn its place. If it doesn't raise margin, it's noise.**

## 2. The 80/20 of Offerings

The **Pareto Principle** applies here too. In most businesses, 20% of products or services generate 80% of profit. The rest are distractions.

Coca-Cola once had hundreds of products, but 70% of revenue still came from Coke itself. By simplifying and focusing marketing, they protected margin while cutting costs.

☞ **Operator's Move: Rank every product/service by profit, not revenue. Kill or bundle the bottom 50%.**

## 3. The Hidden Tax of "Custom Work"

Service businesses bleed from complexity in the form of custom work. Every special request breaks systems, adds errors, and eats margin.

Consultants, agencies, and freelancers often undercharge for custom jobs, forgetting the extra time and overhead required. The result? Invisible margin bleed.

☞ **Operator's Move: Standardize 80% of delivery. Charge a premium for custom — or stop offering it.**

## 4. Simplicity as a Profit Multiplier

Companies that scale profitably usually have a **tight focus:**

- **In-N-Out Burger:** 3 items. High margin, low complexity.
- **Ryanair:** No-frills flights. High utilization, low costs.
- **Apple (early days):** Four products. Maximum clarity, massive margins.

☞ **Operator's Move: Complexity dilutes power. Simplicity concentrates it.**

## 5. The "Profit Line Test"

Run every product/service through this test:

1. Does it produce above-average margin?
2. Does it scale without adding hidden costs?
3. Does it strengthen or weaken our core brand?

☞ **Operator's Move:** If the answer is no → cut it. Complexity is never neutral. It either compounds or corrodes margin.

## 6. Quick Action: Complexity Audit

This week:

1. List every product/service you offer.
2. Rank by **profit margin**, not sales.
3. Kill the bottom 20% or raise their price.
4. Standardize delivery for the top 20%.
5. Track savings in time, labor, and overhead.

*Final words:*

The herd believes more is better. They chase every opportunity, pile on products, and ultimately drown in their own chaos.

The wolf knows better. Simplicity is lethal. It's clean, efficient, and sharp. Every layer of complexity is a dull edge. Every cut makes you faster, stronger, more profitable.

Protect your margin by cutting the fat. In the hunt for profit, the sharpest blade always wins.

# 6

# People & Productivity

Payroll is often the single largest expense in any business. Done right, it creates leverage — smart, motivated people who multiply revenue while protecting margin. Done wrong, it becomes dead weight — bloated payroll, endless inefficiency, and hidden costs that bleed you dry.

The herd hires fast, manages weakly, and pays for busywork. Wolves hire slow, manage tight, and reward results. This chapter is about shifting your team from a cost center to a profit engine.

## 1. Labor as Leverage

A-players aren't an expense. They're assets. One top performer often produces as much as three average employees. That's not theory — a McKinsey study found **high performers are up to 400% more productive** than average ones.

☞ **Operator's Move: Hire fewer, better people. Pay them more,**

**expect more, and cut dead weight early.**

## 2. The Hidden Costs of C-Players

Keeping weak performers isn't neutral — it actively destroys margin. They:

- Slow projects.
- Drain manager time.
- Lower team morale.
- Force A-players to pick up slack (leading to burnout).

Netflix's **"keeper test"** solves this: if a manager wouldn't fight to keep someone, they let them go. Ruthless? Yes. But margin thrives under clarity.

☞ **Operator's Move: Apply the keeper test quarterly. Don't carry dead weight.**

## 3. Incentives That Protect Margin

Most companies misalign incentives. They reward activity, not results. A salesperson gets paid for calls, not closed deals. A manager gets rewarded for headcount growth, not margin growth.

☞ **Operator's Move: Tie incentives directly to margin drivers.**

- Sales → % of profitable revenue, not just top-line.
- Managers → bonuses tied to efficiency gains.
- Teams → rewards for cutting costs, improving processes, or increasing yield.

When pay matches profit, behavior follows.

## 4. Time Discipline

Labor isn't just about headcount. It's about time. A business full of "busy" people still burns margin if that time doesn't create value.

Harvard Business Review found that employees waste **23 hours a week in unproductive meetings.** That's over half a workweek.

☞ **Operator's Move:**

- Cut recurring meetings unless they prove ROI.
- Track output, not hours.
- Default to async updates.

Time = margin. Protect it ruthlessly.

## 5. The Power of Training

Training is often seen as a cost, but it's margin insurance. Employees without training make errors, repeat mistakes, and waste resources. Microsoft found that structured onboarding improved employee productivity by **50% in the first 6 months.**

☞ **Operator's Move: Create lean SOPs and training materials. Every hour spent training upfront saves dozens later.**

## 6. Outsourcing & Automation

Not every role belongs in-house. Some tasks are cheaper and more efficient when outsourced or automated. Payroll, IT, and customer support — all can often be done better and cheaper outside.

☞ **Operator's Move: Ask: *Is this task core to our margin engine?* If not, outsource or automate.**

## 7. Quick Action: Team Margin Audit

This week:

1. List every team member and their cost.
2. Write their #1 contribution to margin.
3. If it's unclear → red flag.

4. Rank by margin contribution → top 20% are A-players, bottom 20% are risks.
5. Adjust roles, incentives, or cuts accordingly.

*Final words:*

The herd hires for comfort. They keep people around because it's easy, not because it's profitable. Wolves hire for leverage. They demand results. They cut fast, reward strong, and align everyone to margin.

Because in the hunt for profit, dead weight slows you down. A lean, sharp pack wins every time.

# 7

# Tech & Automation

Technology is either your sharpest weapon or your heaviest anchor. Most businesses treat tools as toys — stacking subscriptions and shiny apps that add cost but not profit. Operators treat technology as leverage — stripping away overhead, speeding execution, and scaling margin without adding headcount.

## 1. The True Role of Tech

Tech isn't meant to impress your team. It's meant to **replace cost and amplify output.** Every tool you pay for should either:

- Reduce time.
- Reduce headcount.
- Increase margin.

☞ **Operator's Move: For each tool, ask: *Does this cut cost or multiply efficiency?* If not, cut it.**

## 2. The Trap of Tool Creep

The average SMB now uses over **100 SaaS tools.** Most overlap, creating chaos and cost. Tool sprawl eats margin silently.

☞ **Operator's Move: Consolidate. One CRM, one project tool, one communication channel. Less is cheaper, faster, and cleaner.**

## 3. Automation = Hidden Margin

Every repetitive task left manual bleeds profit. Payroll, invoicing, lead routing, and customer follow-ups — all can be automated. McKinsey estimates automation can cut **30% of operational costs** for SMBs.

☞ **Operator's Move: Automate one recurring process per quarter. Each automation compounds over time.**

## 4. The AI Advantage

AI is no longer optional. It can:

- Draft sales copy.
- Analyze cash flows.

- Run customer support at scale.
- Predict demand and inventory.

The businesses adopting AI now are widening their margin gap while the herd hesitates.

**☞ Operator's Move: Audit your top 5 workflows. Where can AI cut time in half?**

## 5. Quick Action: Tech Hygiene

1. Audit all tools.
2. Cut or consolidate low-ROI apps.
3. Automate one major process.
4. Test one AI tool for core business function.

*Final words:*

Tech isn't about being trendy. It's about leverage. The herd chases apps. Wolves weaponize them.

Every automation is a margin booster. Every cut in complexity is a sharper edge. Don't play with tools. Wield them.

# 8

# The Audit Framework

You can't protect what you don't measure. The businesses with the strongest margins aren't always the flashiest — they're the most disciplined. They run **profit audits** regularly, like health checkups, catching leaks before they grow.

## 1. Why Audits Win

Margin erosion is silent. Without audits, you only notice when it's too late. Operators don't wait — they track, measure, and adjust quarterly.

## 2. The Audit Playbook

Every quarter, run this:

1. **Revenue Audit** – Which customers, products, or services actually drive profit?
2. **Expense Audit** – Which costs are growing without ROI?
3. **Process Audit** – Which workflows are slow, redundant, or error-prone?
4. **Team Audit** – Who multiplies efficiency? Who drains it?
5. **Tool Audit** – Which subscriptions are unused or redundant?

☞ **Operator's Move: Treat audits as non-negotiable.**

## 3. The KPI Dashboard

You need real-time visibility. Core KPIs:

- Gross margin %
- Net margin %
- Cash conversion cycle
- CAC/LTV
- Payroll % of revenue

☞ **Operator's Move: Review weekly. If a KPI trends negatively, act immediately.**

## 4. External Eyes

Sometimes you're too close to the business to see leaks. Use outside consultants, accountants, or peer groups for fresh audits. Amazon hires "red teams" to test their assumptions.

☞ **Operator's Move: Bring in outside eyes once a year.**

## 5. Quick Action: Audit in 7 Days

- Day 1–2: Expense review.
- Day 3: Margin per product/service.
- Day 4: Team review.
- Day 5: Tools & subscriptions.
- Day 6: Cash flow map.
- Day 7: Decide top 3 fixes.

*Final words:*

The herd runs blindly until disaster. Wolves track every move, every leak, every margin line. Audits aren't optional — they're survival.

# 9

# Case Studies: Unlocking Hidden Profits

Theory is easy to dismiss. Numbers are not. Case studies prove that invisible margin isn't abstract — it's real, measurable, and accessible.

These aren't billion-dollar corporations with endless resources. They're everyday operators — retailers, freelancers, agencies, restaurants — who discovered hidden profit by changing how they think and act. The results were staggering.

## 1. The Retailer Who Cut SKUs

A mid-sized retail chain carried over 3,000 products. But an internal audit revealed something shocking: **80% of profit came from just 300 items.** The other 2,700 were tying up cash in inventory, requiring extra storage, and complicating logistics.

By eliminating low-margin SKUs, they freed up **$2M in working capital** and reduced warehousing costs by 25%. Customers didn't complain — in fact, sales increased because choice overload disappeared.

☞ **Lesson: More isn't better. More is a trap. Streamlined offerings improve both customer clarity and margin.**

## 2. The Agency That Automated

A 12-person digital marketing agency wasted **20 hours per week** preparing client reports. That's the equivalent of a full-time employee generating zero margin.

By building automated dashboards (Google Data Studio + Zapier), they cut reporting time by 90%. That freed up 80 hours/month, equal to $4,000 in hidden labor costs. They didn't lay people off — they reassigned them to higher-value activities like upselling clients.

☞ **Lesson: Automation doesn't cut jobs. It frees talent to create margin.**

## 3. The SaaS That Raised Prices

A software startup charged $29/month for its platform. They feared raising prices would scare customers away. After analysis, they switched to a **tiered pricing model**:

- $49 Basic

- $99 Pro
- $199 Enterprise

Result: churn stayed the same. 35% of new customers chose the $99 tier. Annual recurring revenue jumped 40% with no new marketing spend.

☞ **Lesson: Underpricing is self-sabotage. Value-based pricing can transform profit instantly.**

## 4. The Restaurant That Fixed Waste

One restaurant lost thousands each month to food spoilage. By installing inventory software and retraining staff on portion control, they reduced waste by **20%.**

That alone added $75,000 in annual margin — equal to hiring another cook without actually paying one.

☞ **Lesson: Waste is a profit killer. Cutting it is as valuable as selling more.**

## 5. The Freelancer Who Standardized

A designer offered unlimited custom packages. Clients demanded revisions endlessly, often beyond the scope of what they paid.

She created **3 fixed packages**: Starter, Growth, and Premium.

Delivery became 50% faster, clients were clearer on expectations, and margin per project doubled. Burnout disappeared because the scope was controlled.

☞ **Lesson: Standardization multiplies efficiency and protects margin.**

## 6. The Manufacturer Who Negotiated Terms

A mid-sized manufacturer had 45-day receivables but 30-day payables. That gap created constant cash strain, forcing them into expensive short-term loans.

By renegotiating supplier contracts to net-45, they unlocked $500,000 in working capital. No loans needed. That saved $50,000 annually in interest.

☞ **Lesson: Float is an invisible margin. Negotiate terms to protect cash.**

*Final words:*

The herd thinks "profit" comes from more sales. Wolves know profit comes from **control.** Every business above unlocked hidden profit without chasing new customers. They cut leaks, raised prices, simplified offers, and controlled cash.

That's the invisible margin — waiting in your business right now.

# 10

# The Ruthless Operator

At the end of the hunt, tools and tactics only work if the operator has the right mindset. This chapter isn't about numbers — it's about discipline. The wolf's way of thinking.

## 1. Profit Is Oxygen

You can't survive without oxygen. Businesses can't survive without a margin. Revenue keeps the ego alive. Margin keeps the company alive.

Operators never sacrifice margin for vanity. They would rather grow slower with discipline than grow faster and bleed to death.

☞ **Rule: Protect margin at all costs.**

## 2. Discipline Over Ego

The herd confuses "looking successful" with being successful. Fancy offices, bloated teams, endless product lines — they chase appearances.

Operators focus on substance. Bezos famously kept Amazon desks made from doors long after IPO. Why? Because vanity kills discipline, and discipline builds empires.

☞ **Rule: Ego spends. Operators compound.**

## 3. Ruthless Simplicity

Every layer of complexity is a leak. Every cut is a gain. Wolves cut fat without hesitation.

Apple nearly collapsed in the 1990s under too many products. Jobs returned, cut 70% of the line, and focused on four winners. The rest is history.

☞ **Rule: Simplify until it hurts — then simplify more.**

## 4. The 90-Day Profit Cycle

Operators don't wait for disaster. Every 90 days, they:

- Audit expenses.
- Review team performance.

- Reevaluate pricing.
- Kill or streamline low-margin products.
- Reinvest in what compounds.

Discipline compounds. Every cycle makes the machine tighter, faster, more profitable.

☞ **Rule: Never coast. Hunt quarterly.**

## 5. Operator vs. Herd

- **The herd:** Chases revenue, ignores leaks, carries dead weight, prays for growth.
- **The operator:** Hunts profit, patches leaks, cuts fat, compounds discipline.

The herd survives when times are good. Operators survive **always.**

## 6. Building the Wolf's Edge

The wolf's edge isn't aggression. It's clarity. It's the discipline to cut distractions, the focus to guard margin, the ruthlessness to stay lean when others get bloated.

That's what separates survivors from prey. And that's what will separate you.

*Final words:*

*Profit is sanity. Margin is survival. Discipline is freedom.*

The herd will always chase vanity. They'll always bleed. They'll always fail.

But you won't. You've read the map. You've built the systems. You've sharpened your edge.

Now it's simple: protect the margin. Multiply the margin. Own the margin.

Because in the end, the ruthless operator always eats first.

# 11

# Customer Lifetime Value: The Overlooked Goldmine

Most businesses chase new customers like addicts. They burn money on ads, discounts, and promotions, all to bring in more people through the door. But here's the truth: the most profitable customers are the ones you already have.

This is where **Customer Lifetime Value (LTV)** comes in. It measures how much a customer is worth to you over the entire relationship — not just the first sale. And when you understand LTV, you stop chasing vanity growth and start capturing invisible profit.

## 1. Why LTV Matters More Than Sales

Acquiring new customers is expensive. According to Harvard Business Review, it costs **5–25x more** to acquire a new customer than to keep an existing one. Bain & Company found that increasing retention rates by just **5%** can boost profits by

**25–95%.**

☞ Operator's Move: If your LTV isn't growing, your profit isn't compounding.

## 2. How to Calculate LTV

The simple formula:

**LTV = (Average Purchase Value × Purchase Frequency × Customer Lifespan) – Acquisition Cost**

Example:

- Average order = $100
- Buys 4 times per year = $400/year
- Stays for 5 years = $2,000 total
- CAC (cost to acquire) = $300
- ☞ **LTV = $1,700**

☞ Operator's Move: If you don't know your LTV, you're flying blind. Start tracking it this quarter.

## 3. Unlocking LTV

The herd focuses on one-time sales. Wolves engineer systems that stretch customer value over years.

### 🔑 *Strategies to Boost LTV:*

1. **Retention programs:** Loyalty rewards, memberships, exclusive perks.
2. **Upsells:** Offer higher-value packages at the point of sale.
3. **Cross-sells:** Sell complementary products/services.
4. **Recurring revenue:** Subscription models create predictable LTV.
5. **Customer experience:** A smooth experience keeps them coming back.

👉 Example: Amazon Prime. A $139 annual subscription massively increases customer loyalty and purchase frequency.

## 4. The Churn Factor

Churn (losing customers) is the LTV killer. A business with 20% churn must constantly replace one-fifth of its base just to stand still.

👉 Operator's Move: Track churn monthly. Interview lost customers. Fix the top 2 reasons they leave. Lower churn = instant LTV boost.

## 5. Case Study: SaaS Retention

A SaaS company spent heavily on ads to add customers at $200 CAC. Churn was 15% per month — meaning the average customer lasted less than 7 months. LTV was only $500.

By adding onboarding tutorials, live support, and loyalty discounts, churn dropped to 5%. Average customer lifespan doubled. LTV jumped to $1,200. Profit tripled without adding a single new customer.

## 6. Quick Action: LTV Playbook

1. Calculate your current LTV.
2. Identify your top 20% of customers (highest spend, longest loyalty).
3. Create a program just for them — rewards, upsells, exclusives.
4. Track churn. Focus on one fix to lower it.
5. Add at least one recurring revenue stream.

*Final words:*

The herd chases new customers. Wolves grow the ones they already have.

LTV is an invisible margin hiding in plain sight. It's cheaper, faster, and more powerful than any ad campaign. The longer and deeper you keep a customer, the stronger your profit engine becomes.

Stop chasing. Start compounding. That's how wolves turn customers into lifelong assets.

# 12

# The Silent Power of Negotiation

Profit isn't just earned. It's negotiated.

Every supplier contract, lease agreement, payment term, and even customer deal contains hidden room for margin. But most business owners accept the first number they're given. The wolves don't. They negotiate every detail — quietly, consistently, and without apology. That's why they always walk away with more.

## 1. Why Negotiation Is Invisible Profit

Most entrepreneurs obsess over sales and marketing while ignoring costs. But every $1 saved in negotiation is equal to **$1 in pure profit.** Unlike revenue, which requires overhead and fulfillment, negotiation savings go straight to the bottom line.

☞ Operator's Move: Treat negotiation as a **profit lever, not a chore.**

## 2. The Terms Game

Price isn't the only thing negotiable. In fact, **terms often matter more than numbers.**

- **Payment terms:** Net-30 vs Net-60 can free up massive cash flow.
- **Volume discounts:** Committing to steady orders secures better rates.
- **Delivery terms:** Faster, cheaper shipping protects cash cycles.
- **Renewals:** Locking in long-term contracts avoids surprise hikes.

☞ Case: A manufacturer shifted supplier terms from net-30 to net-60. That unlocked **$500k in working capital** without borrowing a dollar.

## 3. How to Negotiate Without Burning Bridges

Negotiation isn't war. Done well, it strengthens relationships.

🗝? *Framework:*

1. **Do your homework:** Know market rates and competitor terms.
2. **Anchor high:** Start with an ask beyond what you expect.

3. **Trade, don't take:** Give something in return (longer contract, volume commitment).
4. **Stay silent:** Don't rush to fill pauses. Silence creates leverage.
5. **Always be willing to walk:** The strongest position is the ability to leave.

☞ Operator's Move: Aim to make every deal **win-win**, but never accept terms that weaken margin.

## 4. Internal Negotiation

Negotiation isn't just with suppliers — it's also with employees, partners, and even customers.

- **Employees:** Negotiate roles, expectations, and incentives tied to margin.
- **Partners:** Align equity splits or profit shares that reward efficiency.
- **Customers:** Push for upfront payments, deposits, or minimum orders.

☞ Operator's Move: Train your entire team in negotiation basics. Profit protection becomes cultural.

## 5. The Psychology of Power in Negotiation

Harvard research shows **confidence and preparation outweigh raw bargaining power.** Wolves don't bluff — they walk in with facts, alternatives, and clarity.

☞ Example: When one supplier quoted a SaaS company a 20% price hike, the founder calmly presented competitor quotes, plus a multi-year renewal offer. Result: the supplier not only held rates but gave a 5% discount.

## 6. Quick Action: Negotiation Audit

This month:

1. List your top 5 expenses (suppliers, rent, software, contractors).
2. Research market benchmarks.
3. Approach each for a negotiation — price, terms, or extras.
4. Even a **5% improvement** across expenses could equal thousands in new profit.

*Final words:*

The herd pays sticker price. Wolves never do.

Negotiation is invisible profit — it requires no marketing, no scaling, no customers. Just discipline, clarity, and courage. Every contract you sign is either protecting or bleeding margin.

The herd avoids negotiation because it feels uncomfortable. The wolf embraces it — because survival is more important than comfort.

# 13

# Anti-Fragile Profit: Thriving in Downturns

Recessions, market crashes, pandemics — downturns are inevitable. Most businesses see them as disasters. But for the operator, downturns are the greatest profit opportunity of all.

Here's why: when pressure hits, the herd panics. They slash prices, cut blindly, and scramble for survival. Wolves tighten discipline, guard margin, and prepare to hunt. Weak competitors collapse, leaving market share and customers up for grabs.

The difference? Anti-fragility. Not just surviving downturns, but using them to get stronger.

## 1. What Anti-Fragile Really Means

Fragile systems break under pressure. Resilient systems survive. **Anti-fragile systems grow.**

Your business should be built so that stress reveals strength, not weakness. That means margin buffers, flexible cost structures, and cash discipline.

☞ Operator's Move: Stop asking *"How do I survive?"* Start asking *"How do I position to grow while others retreat?"*

## 2. Build Margin Buffers

In good times, set aside part of your profit as a margin reserve. This acts like oxygen in a fire. When the herd is gasping, you're breathing.

- Cash reserves cover payroll without panic.
- High margins absorb temporary revenue drops.
- Lean operations prevent collapse under strain.

☞ Example: During the 2008 crash, Costco thrived while competitors drowned. Why? Lean operations and disciplined cash reserves.

## 3. Flexible Cost Structures

The worst mistake is locking yourself into heavy fixed costs. Big offices, bloated payroll, unnecessary debt — these become nooses in downturns.

Operators keep costs flexible:

- More contractors, fewer full-time hires.

- Smaller core offices, remote flexibility.
- Variable marketing spend tied to ROI.

☞ Operator's Move: Keep fixed costs below 40% of revenue. The leaner you are, the harder you are to kill.

## 4. Negotiation in Downturns

Downturns are leverage moments. Suppliers, landlords, and partners get desperate. That's when you renegotiate contracts, leases, and terms to lock in long-term margin.

☞ Example: In 2020, savvy operators secured 20–30% rent reductions simply by asking, because landlords preferred something over vacancy.

## 5. Expand When Others Retreat

The herd cuts marketing, stops hiring, and retreats. Wolves expand strategically. They buy competitors for pennies, hire talent that's suddenly available, and double down on customer acquisition when ad costs drop.

☞ Case: Airbnb scaled during the 2008 crisis by offering cheaper lodging when hotels were collapsing. Uber launched in 2009, seizing the moment when people needed cheaper transport.

## 6. The Anti-Fragile Playbook

1. Build a **margin buffer** (cash + reserves).
2. Keep **costs flexible**, not fixed.
3. Run **quarterly stress tests** (what happens if revenue drops 30%?).
4. Negotiate aggressively in downturns.
5. Be ready to **acquire customers, assets, or competitors** while the herd panics.

*Final words:*

The herd sees downturns as storms to hide from. Wolves see storms as hunting weather.

Every crisis wipes out the fragile and feeds the disciplined. Anti-fragile businesses don't just survive — they expand. They use pressure to sharpen, stress to strengthen, chaos to conquer.

You can't control when the storm comes. But you can control whether it breaks you or makes you. Build your business to thrive in fire — and the herd will never catch you.

# About the Author

Damon Du Bruyn is a young entrepreneur with a sharp eye for systems, strategy, and profit. Having worked with entrepreneurs to streamline operations and boost sales, he's seen firsthand how businesses bleed margin through inefficiency and poor discipline. His mission is simple: expose the leaks most entrepreneurs ignore and teach operators how to protect and multiply profit.

With *The Invisible Margin*, Damon delivers a tool for entrepreneurs who want real results — not vanity metrics. He believes profit isn't just about money — it's about freedom, survival, and building businesses that not only survive, but thrive in any economy.

Jordan Anderson is an entrepreneur passionate about helping

businesses uncover the hidden opportunities most people overlook. With a background in sales and growth strategy, he's worked alongside companies to improve efficiency, sharpen execution, and boost their bottom line.

In *The Invisible Margin*, Jordan brings a clear, practical voice to one of the toughest challenges in business: protecting profit. His goal is to give entrepreneurs the tools, systems, and confidence to cut waste, build discipline, and scale smarter — not just bigger.

**You can connect with me on:**

https://sites.google.com/view/damon-du-bruyn/project-page

www.ingramcontent.com/pod-product-compliance
Lightning Source LLC
LaVergne TN
LVHW090430210926
848480LV00002B/765